Preface

When teachers focus on building learning power in their classrooms, the impact on learners can be startling. I've seen this happen in schools across the UK when teachers have begun to think creatively about the ways in which they can help young people become better learners.

We all know that if you put a deep, practical understanding of learning at the heart of what goes on in classrooms, it will have wide-ranging impact on all young people.

This book is the first in a series of practical handbooks stemming from my earlier book, *Building Learning Power*. It is designed to encourage you to think differently about the ways in which you work with students, and to join other teachers who have changed their focus from the narrow fields of attainment and behaviour to the broader horizons of lifelong learning.

As you journey through this book you will build your own capacity to be a learning powered individual and to generate those '101' approaches that are going to work in your classroom. This approach has been tried and tested through the extensive development work I have been doing with many teachers over the last ten years.

You know that putting learning at the heart of what you do makes sense. We know that Building Learning Power works.

Professor Guy Claxton

Programme Consultant for
Building Learning Power

Introduction

This handbook is written for classroom teachers who have been introduced to the idea of learning power, and who are interested in using it in practice. Ideally, they will have read Guy Claxton's *Building Learning Power*, key concepts of which are summarised very briefly on pages 4 to 7 of this handbook.

You will not find a list of detailed tricks and tips; this is not an instruction manual. The process of building learning power is far too dynamic for that. We are inviting you to make a step change in what you are trying to effect in the classroom. There *are* lists, and classroom examples, and suggestions, but most of these aim to encourage you to expand your own thinking about how you can help young people to become better learners.

Although there are no shortcuts, there are things you can do immediately that will develop learning dispositions and make teaching more rewarding. Successfully fostering the habits needed for lifelong learning takes a little longer!

A tricky choice. Learning power works for all ages, and this handbook applies equally to primary and secondary classrooms. However, where primary school teachers tend to refer to their young learners as pupils, secondary school teachers prefer the term students: whichever word an author picks, she risks offending half of her potential readers. In this handbook we have plumped for 'students': the learning power model treats young people as our active co-participants in the processes of learning, and — whatever the reality in the classroom — the connotations of 'student' perhaps carry more of this active sense than those of the word 'pupil'.

This last point contains the vital aspect of learning power that takes it forward from earlier approaches to learning to learn. Learning power engages your students consciously with the ideas and processes of their own learning, in the knowledge that learning itself is learnable.

We are grateful to Dr Bill Lucas for his helpful comments on an earlier draft. Our thanks go, too, to Dean Purnell for his work on the design and DTP; and to the students and staff of St Michael on the Mount Primary School, Bedminster Down School and Cotham School in Bristol who appear in the photographs in this book.

The Authors

Maryl Chambers and Graham Powell have spearheaded the development of TLO Limited's Building Learning Power programme, helping to bring Guy Claxton's ground-breaking work to schools and teachers.

Maryl is one of the founders of TLO, where she has applied her wide experience of designing learning-focused training to creating and developing the innovative programmes for which the company is renowned. She is co-author of many of TLO's publications.

Graham has been headteacher of a large comprehensive school, and a Senior Adviser and Inspector with Gloucestershire LEA. Since becoming a Principal Consultant with TLO in September 2000, he has specialised in applying innovative coaching methods in professional development. He is co-author of several of TLO's handbooks, including the very successful *Pathways to Coaching*.

Guy Claxton is an internationally acclaimed writer, consultant, lecturer and academic, specialising in creativity, education and the mind. He is Visiting Professor of Learning Science at the University of Bristol's Graduate School of Education, and a Fellow of the British Psychological Society. He has written extensively on subjects from creative thinking to Buddhism, by way of the uses and value of uncertainty in learning, and what it is that makes people effective lifelong learners.

Ideas for using this handbook

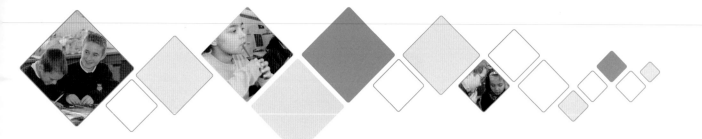

What is learning power?

An approach to learning to learn

Lifelong learning is our birthright. We can continually develop our portable capacity to learn in new and challenging circumstances throughout our lives.

In the developing field of learning to learn, research suggests that there are several broad dispositions that we need to develop in order to become successful lifelong learners.

Guy Claxton, in his book *Building Learning Power*, suggests that there are four key *learning dispositions* – Resilience, Resourcefulness, Reflectiveness and Reciprocity, the new four Rs of learning. These dispositions are inherent in us all. But they are not fixed at birth, or when we leave school: they can be developed by everyone regardless of 'ability', social background, or age. There are no limits to extending our learning power.

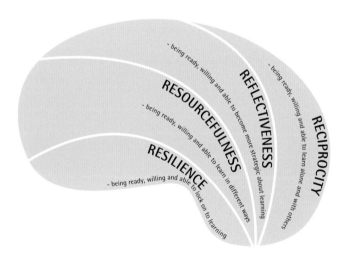

We can think of the dispositions as being like groups of 'learning muscles'. Just as we can build our physical muscles by the right kinds of exercise, so we can exercise our learning muscles to develop their strength and stamina. Developing the dispositions that make for success as a lifelong learner equates to achieving a good level of all-round learning fitness.

Each of the dispositions – the four Rs – is made up of a number of learning behaviours, which we call *learning capacities*. These are summarised on the page opposite. Because the learning capacities are specific in nature, they can be individually trained, nurtured and exercised.

Resilience

is being ready, willing and able to lock onto learning – knowing how to work through difficulties when the pressure mounts or the going gets tough.

Your resilience is made up of . . .

Resourcefulness

is being ready, willing and able to learn in different ways – using both internal and external resources effectively, calling on different ways of learning as appropriate.

Your resourcefulness is made up of . . .

Reflectiveness

is being ready, willing and able to become more strategic about learning – taking a longer-term view by planning, taking stock, and drawing out your experiences as a learner to get the best out of yourself.

Your reflectiveness is made up of . . .

Reciprocity

in learning is being ready, willing and able to learn alone or with other people – using a sense of independent judgement together with skills in communication and empathy.

Your reciprocity is made up of . . .

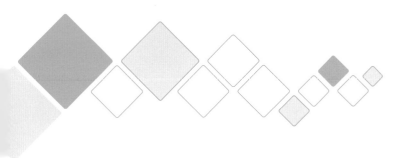

Absorption

Being able to lose yourself in learning — becoming absorbed in what you are doing; rapt and attentive, in a state of 'flow'.

Managing distractions

Recognising and reducing distractions; knowing when to walk away and refresh yourself. Creating your own best environment for learning.

Noticing

Perceiving subtle nuances, patterns and details in experience.

Perseverance

Keeping going in the face of difficulties, channelling the energy of frustration productively. Knowing what a slow and uncertain process learning often is.

Questioning

Asking questions of yourself and others. Being curious and playful with ideas — delving beneath the surface of things.

Making links

Seeing connections between disparate events and experiences — building patterns — weaving a web of understanding.

Imagining

Using your imagination and intuition to put yourself through new experiences or to explore possibilities. Wondering 'what if...?'

Reasoning

Calling up your logical and rational skills to work things out methodically and rigorously; constructing good arguments, and spotting the flaws in others.

Capitalising

Drawing on the full range of resources from the wider world — other people, books, the Internet, past experience, future opportunities ...

Planning

Thinking about where you are going, the action you are going to take, the time and resources you will need, and the obstacles you may encounter.

Revising

Being flexible, changing your plans in the light of different circumstances, monitoring and reviewing how things are going and seeing new opportunities.

Distilling

Looking at what is being learned — pulling out the essential features — carrying them forward to aid further learning; being your own learning coach.

Meta-learning

Knowing yourself as a learner — how you learn best; how to talk about the learning process.

Interdependence

Knowing when it's appropriate to learn on your own or with others, and being able to stand your ground in debate.

Collaboration

Knowing how to manage yourself in the give and take of a collaborative venture, respecting and recognising other view points; adding to and drawing from the strength of teams.

Empathy & listening

Contributing to others' experiences by listening to them to understand what they are really saying, and putting yourself in their shoes.

Imitation

Constructively adopting methods, habits or values from other people whom you observe.

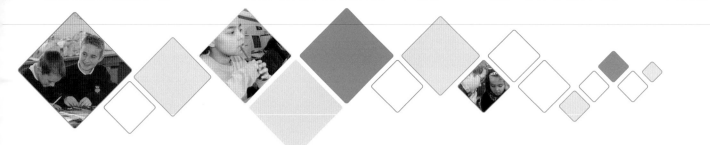

How teachers build learning power

The teacher's palette

As a teacher, you can build young people's learning power by helping them to expand their own learning capacities. This involves the ways in which you talk to students, organise your classroom, and design activities, as well as how you actually teach. It is useful to distinguish four broad ways in which you might work with your students, illustrated in the teaching palette below.

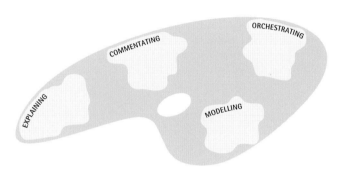

Each of the four main modes of the teaching palette involves a range of behaviours that you can use to support and challenge young learners. The opposite page shows one way of describing these ranges.

Underlying all these approaches is the conscious engagement of teachers and students with the detailed practice of learning to learn. The classroom becomes a place where they engage together creatively as researchers in their own learning.

Explaining

You are overt about learning dispositions by introducing learners directly and explicitly to the four Rs of learning power, and training students in how to use them.

Explaining is made up of...

Orchestrating

You orchestrate resources, the environment and activities in order to develop learning dispositions. Your schemes of work are written with the four Rs in mind, and each learning activity is designed to enhance one or more of the learning capacities.

Orchestrating is made up of...

Commentating

You commentate on your students' learning power through informal talk and formal or informal evaluations. You draw attention to the progress they have made, and to further action that they could take to build learning capacities.

Commentating is made up of...

Modelling

Above all, you model being a learner. You encourage a collective commitment to learning by getting stuck, trying things out, making mistakes, etc. – in the same way as your students. The shared experience is contagious.

Modelling is made up of...

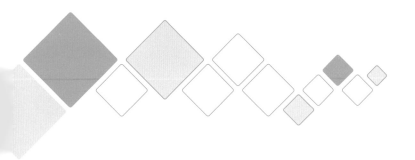

Informing

Providing information about the overall purpose of learning in the classroom and about what learning power consists of, and how it grows.

Reminding

Drawing attention to and prompting about specific aspects of learning power at regular intervals; keeping the ideas fresh.

Discussing

Discussing how to develop learning power and inviting contributions to principles and practices that will inform classroom culture; sharing the inquiry with students.

Training

Directing ways to build learning capacities through specific tips and techniques; inviting critical reflection, and customising.

Selecting

Choosing ways of working and designing activities that will encourage and enhance both curriculum content and learning power.

Framing

Clarifying the learning power expectations behind all classroom activities, in collaboration with students.

Target setting

Helping learners set and monitor their own targets for improving their learning power; using and improving self-evaluation.

Arranging

Deploying the resources and arranging the environment in ways that support the development of learning power; making creative use of space and time.

Nudging

Asking exploratory questions that skilfully move learners onwards in developing themselves as learners. 'How come?', 'What if?', 'How else'?

Replying

Providing written or spoken feedback that encourages further explorations in learning.

Evaluating

Commenting on learning and its outcomes in ways that encourage students to develop the habit of self-evaluation and the creation of targets.

Tracking

Capturing the progress each student makes in developing their learning power over time.

Reacting

Responding to the unexpected with curiosity — saying you don't know and not feeling you have to be the infallible fount of all knowledge.

Learning aloud

Encouraging learners' willingness to explore and tolerate uncertainty by learning and thinking in front of the class.

Demonstrating

Showing that your learning includes diverse activities such as drafting, experimenting, sketching and reflecting.

Sharing

Showing you value learning and are confident in yourself as a learner by sharing your past and present learning endeavours with your learners.

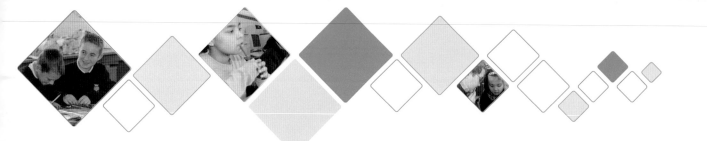

Get curious about your own learning power

Getting to know your learning mind

The best place to start working on learning power is with yourself. As a curious and inquisitive teacher you know that self-observation is the best starting point for challenging and supporting learning capacities in students. So you might think first about how you are as a resilient, resourceful, reflective and reciprocal learner. Use the questions below to look at yourself in relation to the seventeen aspects of a supple learning mind.

Slow down and take time

Make your judgements honestly and openly.

Think about the degree to which you exercise your learning capacities at different times.

Dig a bit deeper, and push yourself to look at the ways in which your learning mind works.

- When are you most able to thrive in each of these aspects?
- Do the answers vary according to circumstances, people, or times of day?
- When have you experienced difficulties?
- What have you done, or could you do, to address those?

Note down what you have learned about your own learning capacities.

		Rarely	Sometimes, or in some circumstances	Always, across the board
1.	When I'm learning, I get completely absorbed	☐	☐	☐
2.	I can shut out distractions when I'm learning	☐	☐	☐
3.	I pay really close attention to the world around me	☐	☐	☐
4.	I stick with my learning, even when I find it hard	☐	☐	☐
5.	My head is full of questions	☐	☐	☐
6.	When I learn, I look for links to what I already know	☐	☐	☐
7.	I see things in my mind's eye when I'm learning	☐	☐	☐
8.	I think carefully and methodically when I'm learning	☐	☐	☐
9.	I make good use of the resources around me when I'm learning	☐	☐	☐
10.	I plan my learning carefully	☐	☐	☐
11.	I keep track of how I am learning as I go along	☐	☐	☐
12.	I think about my learning afterwards to see how I could have gone about it better	☐	☐	☐
13.	I think about how I am changing as a learner	☐	☐	☐
14.	I know when I learn best with others, and when by myself	☐	☐	☐
15.	I work well as part of a team	☐	☐	☐
16.	I readily see things from other people's points of view	☐	☐	☐
17.	I watch other people and pick up their learning habits	☐	☐	☐
18.		☐	☐	☐
19.		☐	☐	☐
20.		☐	☐	☐

For 18, 19 and 20, we invite you to insert other aspects of your learning power that you think are important, but which we may not have covered. We want you always to be thinking critically and creatively about suggestions we make.

What do you believe about learning?

Now think about what you believe about good learners.

Mull over the statements and indicate whether you broadly agree or disagree with them.

Think about how you teach, in relation to each statement. To what extent does your teaching style embody what you say about good learning?

Do you (sometimes) act as if you believed something different from what you say you believe? (This can be a bit uncomfortable!)

		Agree	Disagree
1.	Good learners find learning easy	☐	☐
2.	Good learners are always well organised	☐	☐
3.	Good learners never give up	☐	☐
4.	The best learners are totally independent	☐	☐
5.	Good learners don't make many mistakes	☐	☐
6.	Being a good learner is about how much you know	☐	☐
7.	Good learners are very logical	☐	☐
8.	There is usually one best way to learn	☐	☐
9.	Self-esteem is the most important influence on learning	☐	☐
10.	Success at school means you are a good real-life learner	☐	☐

Research into how we learn has produced much information about the characteristics of successful learners and their ways of learning.

All learners sometimes find learning difficult; it can be messy and confusing, and often defies detailed planning. Good learners are able to work independently, but they also rely on learning with and from other people — including teachers. They know when to give up: at least for the time being, until they find a suitable resource to help combat the difficulty. They make plenty of mistakes, but are always on the look-out for ways to learn from them.

Being a good learner is not about how much you know, more about how you go about getting to know more. It involves being able to learn in multifarious and complicated ways, using intuition and imagination as much as reasoning skills. Learning is not just a matter of skill, it involves personality and values.

Self-esteem alone won't improve learning power; however, help a student become a good learner, and be aware of it, and watch the self-esteem soar.

At present, unfortunately, it is all too common for students to succeed at school without becoming good real-life learners.

Think about how your beliefs about learning relate to these thumbnail characteristics of good learners.

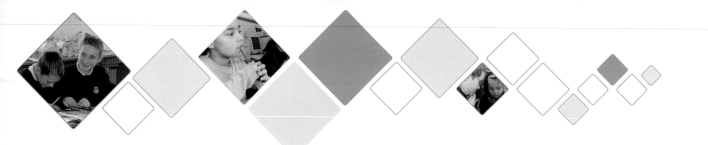

Get curious about your students' learning power

Now turn your attention to the people whose learning you guide and inspire. Look at the following descriptors of aspects of resilience, resourcefulness, reflectiveness and reciprocity. Think about your own students. How well do you know their current strengths and weaknesses as learners?

Try to fill the name of a student into each descriptor, and think what evidence you might have that supports this judgement.

Now analyse your answers. Are there students in the class who are not mentioned? Where might you place them? Is there a gender imbalance in the students you have named?

Are the named students mostly high or low attainers, or do they represent a range of attainment? What other questions does your list of answers raise?

You may find it interesting to think of students who don't like a challenge, or don't work well with others, or don't look to see how things fit together. But remember, those attitudes and behaviours are not set for all time. Helping students develop better learning habits — coaching them to flex and strengthen their learning muscles — is what building learning power is about.

Resilience in my students

- _____ likes a challenge
- _____ is not afraid of finding things hard
- _____ gets 'lost' in learning
- _____ makes accurate descriptions and observations
- _____ minimises negative distractions
- _____ sticks at things despite difficulties

Reflectiveness in my students

- _____ sorts out what needs to be done
- _____ likes to organise their work
- _____ takes stock to make sure things are on track
- _____ anticipates blocks & obstacles
- _____ pulls out key points from experience
- _____ can talk about their learning process

Resourcefulness in my students

- _____ is curious about possibilities
- _____ likes to get to the bottom of things
- _____ likes to see how things fit together
- _____ is logical and systematic when necessary
- _____ makes the most of a range of learning resources
- _____ enjoys using imagination

Reciprocity in my students

- _____ works well with others
- _____ maintains own ideas in a group
- _____ knows when to learn alone and when with others
- _____ shares ideas and information
- _____ puts themselves in other people's shoes
- _____ learns from the way other people do things

What do you believe about learning?

Now that you have got a feel for your students' learning habits, why not ask them what they think? You could use the same questionnaire as you used on page 8, or make up one of your own. The statements alongside offer some more ideas for enquiring about learning power. You may want to add other aspects of the four Rs, or adapt the language to your students' age range.

You could introduce your questionnaire to students by saying something like:

- 'Above all, school is about helping you to know how to strengthen the ways in which you learn – learning how to learn is something that you will need for the rest of your lives.'
- 'This is not a test, but a way of looking at how you see yourself as a learner now.'
- 'Your answers will help you and me to see which learning habits could be strengthened'.
- 'There are no right answers, only your own honest answers.'

Asking students to reflect on the ways in which they learn provides useful data for you. It also raises their awareness about your prime commitment in the classroom.

How much do you agree or disagree with each of the statements?
(Answer 1: Strongly disagree 2: Disagree 3: Agree 4: Strongly agree)

A I know what to do when I get stuck with my work
  1 ☐   2 ☐   3 ☐   4 ☐

B I can concentrate for a long time without being distracted
  1 ☐   2 ☐   3 ☐   4 ☐

C I always plan my work carefully
  1 ☐   2 ☐   3 ☐   4 ☐

D I don't mind if I make a mistake
  1 ☐   2 ☐   3 ☐   4 ☐

E I know where to go to find things out
  1 ☐   2 ☐   3 ☐   4 ☐

F I often ask myself 'what might happen if ...?'
  1 ☐   2 ☐   3 ☐   4 ☐

G I'm good at learning with other people
  1 ☐   2 ☐   3 ☐   4 ☐

H I'm good at picking out the main points at the end of a lesson
  1 ☐   2 ☐   3 ☐   4 ☐

Example 1

Learning power perceptions profile: Lisa G

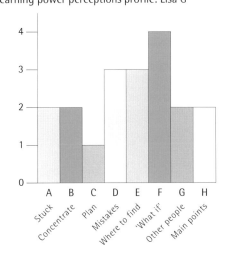

Example 2

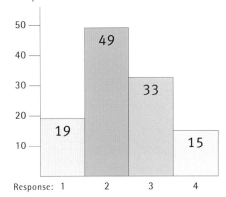

Whole class – 29 students
Four 'Reflectiveness' questions

Looking at the data

Once your students have completed the questionnaire, you can analyse and display the data in a number of ways.

The responses provide a simple but detailed profile of each student's perception of their capacities (Example 1). For a general profile of the class, you could average the students' responses for each question; and you could do the same for various groups of students.

Alternatively, you could focus on particular questions, or groups of related questions (e.g. C and H above are about reflectiveness). A set of histograms of responses will reveal a picture of how different groups within the class perceive their learning – boys and girls, the gifted and talented, those on the register of special educational needs, etc. (Example 2.)

Let the data drive your curiosity. Looking particularly at individuals, are their answers what you would have expected? Where are the surprises? (Look back at what you thought on the facing page!)

Having studied the data, you are in a position to talk with your students about specific aspects of learning power that it would be good to focus on: perhaps some with the whole class, others with groups within the class, and others again with individuals.

Involving your students in this enquiry raises the learning stakes. You could put a class 'learning power profile' on the wall, as part of familiarising your students with the learning capacities. Don't be afraid to invite your students to contribute to this 'research' – designing new questions, developing the four Rs framework, thinking of new ways to aggregate the data. You may be surprised by how creative they are.

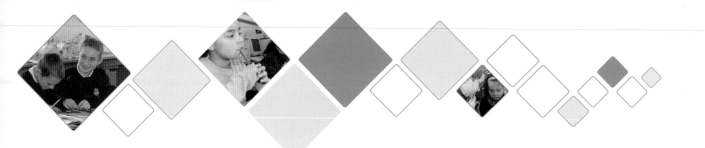

Get curious about boosting your teaching

The statements in the left-hand column are about conventional 'good teaching'. Those in the right-hand column describe what you might be doing when your goal is to boost your students' learning power.

Consider each good teaching statement (column A) and gauge whether you do this sometimes or routinely. Now look at the boosting statements in column B and estimate the extent to which they describe your teaching. Habits like these add an extra dimension to good teaching: you are acting as a learning coach, deliberately working on those learning muscles at the same time as conveying the curriculum message.

A
Good teaching

		Sometimes	Routinely
1A.	My lessons have clear objectives based on a scheme of work	☐	☐
2A.	I am secure and confident in my curriculum knowledge	☐	☐
3A.	Students answer my questions confidently	☐	☐
4A.	I ask questions that encourage exploration of the subject matter	☐	☐
5A.	I show students how to remember things	☐	☐
6A.	I ensure students work together in groups	☐	☐
7A.	I'm always available to help students through a learning challenge	☐	☐
8A.	I build variety and change of pace into lessons	☐	☐
9A.	I mark work regularly with supportive comments and targets	☐	☐
10A.	I display students' best work on classroom walls	☐	☐
11A.	My records show that students make progress with attainment	☐	☐
12A.	I work hard to get things right	☐	☐

B
Boosting learning power

		Sometimes	Routinely
1B.	My students know which learning disposition we are trying to build in each lesson	☐	☐
2B.	I show students that I too am learning in lessons	☐	☐
3B.	I encourage students to ask curious questions of me and each other	☐	☐
4B.	I ask questions which help students explore their learning process	☐	☐
5B.	I guide students to build their capacities to learn	☐	☐
6B.	I help students understand how to learn effectively in groups	☐	☐
7B.	I help students develop their own strategies for coping with being stuck	☐	☐
8B.	I vary methods of working in order to develop different learning capacities	☐	☐
9B.	My marking poses questions about students' progress as learners	☐	☐
10B.	I display work in progress on classroom walls	☐	☐
11B.	I chart progress in the development of learning capacities with my students	☐	☐
12B.	I learn from my mistakes with my students	☐	☐

Scoring your answers

For each 'sometimes' answer, in left- or right-hand column, score 1; for each 'routinely' answer score 2. Enter your combined score for an A–B pair of questions in the appropriate box below, and total the scores for each group of three pairs (the result should be in the range 6 to 12).

		Questions / scores			Total score
Explaining	You explain to students how they learn, and how they can learn to become better learners	1: ☐	5: ☐	6: ☐	☐
Orchestrating	Your classroom and learning activities are organised to help develop your students' learning power	7: ☐	8: ☐	10: ☐	☐
Commentating	Feedback and commentary, from you and your students, ensures progress in learning capacities	4: ☐	9: ☐	11: ☐	☐
Modelling	You act as a leading learner, encouraging and modelling learning in practice	2: ☐	3: ☐	12: ☐	☐

What your scores might suggest about your teaching

Explaining question-group

Below 10 - You know what is expected of you as a teacher. You are clear in your approach and provide a secure structure for your students. You have clear expectations that ensure good progress in attainment. You show your students how they can improve.

10 or above - You provide scaffolding to support students' learning. You are overt about learning to learn, and enable students to strengthen their learning dispositions. Everyone knows what s/he is trying to achieve, in their learning power as well as in response to the demands of the curriculum.

Orchestrating question-group

Below 10 – You provide a stimulating and supportive classroom environment and lessons that ensure all resources are deployed to support students effectively. Students know that they can depend on you to make things happen for them.

10 or above – Your organisation of the classroom and your lessons consistently focus on learning. You consciously foster independence in learners, who are then able to operate interdependently with yourself and other learners.

Commentating question-group

Below 10 – Your procedures for assessment, recording and reporting are robust. You know how well students are progressing and what they need to do to improve attainment levels. You make sure that assessment supports improvement.

10 or above – You feed back to students about their progress as learners. You know which learning capacities they need to extend, and how they are improving. You pose questions to assist them in developing their learning capacities on their own.

Modelling question-group

Below 10 – Your students are confident in you as a teacher. They know that you can be trusted to provide a safe and supportive classroom and that you know what to do to help them succeed.

10 or above – Your students see you as a committed learner. You demonstrate to them that everyone is learning to learn throughout their lives – in the classroom and beyond. They can see that you are finding out, getting things wrong and learning alongside them.

Building students' learning power is not about doing more, but rather about doing things a little differently. It means boosting your teaching effectiveness by becoming a learning-power coach to your students.

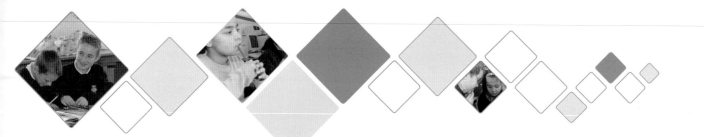

Make a start: Small changes, big levers

So, fostering students' learning capacities is a wide-ranging and multifarious business. However, there are a few straightforward things you can do to start engaging your students in developing their learning dispositions.

You can't do everything at once, but, as many teachers have found, a few changes can have a gratifying and immediate impact on how well your students learn. We call them 'quick wins': they are almost bound to give positive results, and keep you and your students motivated to try more.

The next few pages offer you a wider range of ideas to choose from. These should give an indication of the many ways in which you can help young people learn how to learn.

Remember, the point is to create a learning environment that supports students in extending their own learning power, not just one in which they can demonstrate their current learning power.

Key teacher behaviours (see pages 6 & 7)

Explaining

Be overt about learning to learn. Introduce learners directly and explicitly to the four Rs of learning power, and train learners in how to use them.

Orchestrating

Orchestrate resources, the environment and activities in order to develop students' learning dispositions. Incorporate the four Rs into schemes of work and design learning activities to enhance one or more of the learning dispositions.

Commentating

Commentate on students' learning power through informal talk and formal or informal evaluations. Draw attention to progress made, and to further action that could be taken to strengthen learning dispositions.

Modelling

Model being a learner. Encourage a collective commitment to learning by getting stuck, trying things out, making mistakes, etc. – in the same way as younger learners.

Quick wins

- Explain to students how they will learn better if they develop their 'learning muscles' by regular work-outs.
- Introduce one R each week, but not all of the seventeen capacities at this stage.
- Ask the class to invent characters who illustrate the four Rs.

- Design at least one learning activity each day that aims to develop one of the four Rs as well as a curriculum outcome. Share the twin nature of these activities with your students.
- Display the learning progression of students' work rather than the perfect outcome.

- Explore with students how it feels to be stuck in learning, and develop a list of suggested unsticking strategies.
- Point out to students when they are using one of the four Rs effectively.
- Reward or acknowledge good questions as much as good answers.

- Concentrate on modelling the R that is being introduced; draw attention to how you are doing this.

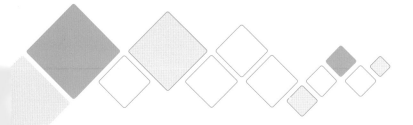

Make a start: Explaining

You might

- start by telling students that being a learner is something that will be with them all their lives and that we can all build our 'learning muscles'
- talk with students about how other people display the four Rs in their everyday life
- consider with the whole class which of the four Rs to start work on
- explore how students think they use each of the four Rs, in school and in their wider lives

and

- design a display to show the importance of learning power for life with some popular role models 'speaking out' on behalf of the four Rs
- provide an unsticking box with cards suggesting strategies to try when the going gets tough
- use the white-board, flip-chart, cards and Post-it notes to capture the class's exploration of their chosen aspect of learning power
- have a blank sheet on the wall, or a suggestions / questions box, to which students can add their learning power ideas or queries

Sarah introduced her class to learning to learn by talking with them about how she has been learning as a teacher, a salsa dancer, a computer illiterate, a daughter, a flat-dweller. She asked them to think about what 'learning muscles' she needed to develop to do some of these things. She matched their suggestions to the four Rs and asked them to think about the times when they used these 'muscles' at school, at home, with friends, at clubs.

They built a list of the things they needed from school if it was to help them become real-life learners. The list included things like time to talk about learning, more helpful comments on work, less direction, more responsibility, work more with other people, more access to the Internet.

Sarah shared some examples of well-known people, and some of the learning obstacles they had overcome.

She was pleased by her students' enthusiasm for the four Rs, so a couple of weeks later she got the class to fill in a learning power questionnaire. They helped to collate and analyse the results as part of an IT session. The survey revealed that they would all benefit from developing greater resourcefulness, and from becoming less dependent on her — more resilient.

As a first step towards building resilience, they developed a flow chart together on 'What to do when we don't know what to do'.

❝ I need to

- undertake some personal research into learning to learn
- look out for topical information about learning and discuss it with my students
- begin to think of myself as a learning coach

and to remember that

- 'Stuckness is OK' and that being stuck should be a site of interest not shame
- any ideas we are working on are 'work in progress' ❞

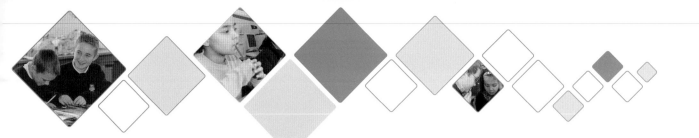

Make a start: Orchestrating

You might

- look at the learning activities for a lesson, a day, a week, and ask yourself which learning capacities the activities will extend as currently designed
- design or redesign learning activities with at least one of the learning capacities in mind
- re-cast learning objectives to include learning-power objectives as well as content objectives
- introduce a twin-objective activity each day, and ensure that every student is clear about the intention behind the dual nature of the activity
- invite students to keep a learning log to help develop their thinking about learning

and

- rearrange the classroom and resources to allow for greater learning flexibility and self-reliance
- provide learning-power prompts on the walls and ceilings, and change them regularly
- display work in progress showing the progression of learning rather than perfect finished products

❝I need to

- keep the environment inspiring, adding new visuals frequently
- provide subliminal prompts – on mouse mats, screen savers, Post-it notes ...
- avoid overdoing my references to the four Rs

and to remember that

- students can act as a learning resource for each other
- I can generate and share new ideas with colleagues ❞

Sarah realised that she needed to refocus her work. She took four highlighter pens and a pile of Post-it notes and combed through her team's current curriculum plans with her colleague, Rashid.

They discovered places where they could be more overt about developing learning power and began to re-cast activities and projects in ways that would capture and develop the learning capacities.

Rashid spent a morning in Sarah's lessons, studying the effectiveness of her classroom for developing learning power. They reorganised resources and furniture to move the focus away from her, and towards encouraging more independence in learning. The new configuration would make Sarah change the way she interacted with the students.

The walls were crying out to be used to support learning power. Current displays showed examples of finished and well-presented work, mixed with bright and eye-catching commercial posters. However, these did not focus attention on exploratory and independent approaches to learning.

Sarah determined to display students' early drafts or first attempts, and add improved drafts and finished pieces of work later. This would be part of getting her students to see learning as a process.

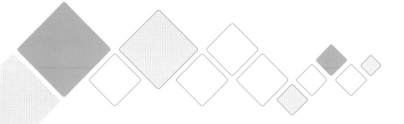

Make a start: Commentating

You might

- focus your comments and encouragement on engagement rather than success
- conduct a survey of each individual's perceived learning power
- develop your vocabulary for talking about learning
- discuss success criteria with a view to enabling students to check their own work
- prompt students to think about which learning capacities they are using to tackle a task, and help them explore others they might use
- make time for students to ask more questions
- encourage students to share their speculative ideas

and

- use a classroom wall as a 'Learning Wall' to display students' own targets and progress in their learning capacities
- develop a list of 'could do' questions which students can use in supporting each other in learning to learn
- start a 'Question Wall' where you and the students can record questions and review them every so often

At first Sarah regularly talked about resilience, resourcefulness, reflectiveness and reciprocity in order to establish these ways of working in the classroom. However, to avoid her class growing tired of hearing the same words repeated, she soon began to introduce the learning capacities explicitly.

She recognised too that she would have to listen better and notice how her students were learning. She needed to train herself to ask the kind of questions that would help them reflect on how they were learning. Rashid coached her on her listening and questioning skills, so that she became better at asking 'could be', 'what if', 'I wonder if' and 'when might' questions.

She gradually became more rigorous and searching in the feedback she provided. Rather than urging her students to 'be resilient ...' she commentated in detail on their work, and on the learning capacities they were using.

She told her students what she was doing, and asked for their help to monitor her and tell her when she lapsed into habits that weren't helpful. This began to equip them to work as learning coaches for each other.

Sarah's students realised that they could set themselves learning-power targets, e.g. to ask better questions, to persevere with a task for longer without help, to notice more details, to try to understand other points of view.

“ I need to

- guide more and tell less
- listen to understand their learning
- find better ways to ask 'why' questions
- use praise appropriately
- develop coaching skills in myself and others

and to remember that

- developing these skills will take time and effort
- adding new ideas bit by bit will be more beneficial and less confusing for students **”**

Make a start: Modelling

You might

- show students that you are learning alongside them in lessons
- talk through the process of solving a problem together, rather than simply presenting the right answer
- make an effort to use 'it could be' and 'it might' language often, rather than the language of certainty
- acknowledge mistakes you make and show that you enjoy learning from them
- invite students to set you challenges that you can work through in front of them

and

- have your own learning project in the classroom that you can work on from time to time and share with students
- at the end of the day or week, use the white-board to make a list of things that you have learnt
- keep your own learning journal and write in it when students write in theirs
- invite other teachers into the classroom to learn with you, and let students know that this is what you are doing

> **❝I need to**
>
> - be genuine and authentic as a learner
> - say 'I'm learning how ...' not 'I can't'
> - learn from the students
> - learn with other colleagues
>
> **and to remember that**
>
> - I don't have to have all the answers **❞**

Sarah knew that the most powerful resource available to her class would be to see their teacher as a learner: getting stuck, trying things out, making mistakes, and making small learning gains. She realised that this wouldn't work unless her approach was seen to be genuine; she would rapidly lose her students' trust if she appeared at all contrived. Using her own experiences in explaining learning power would demonstrate how she was committed to the things she was encouraging her students to do.

For several of her students, getting things wrong and being stuck had been leading to learned helplessness. Sarah had to model in front of them that making mistakes and getting stuck was what everyone did, and that this was OK; and also that what counted was recognising and learning from mistakes, and using a variety of ways to go 'beyond stuck'.

Much of what Sarah wanted her students to achieve depended on greater reflection about learning, so she decided that she would steadfastly do those reflective things alongside them. As a start, she told them how, after each day at school, she thought about what had happened and what she had learned. Yesterday, she had learned that ...

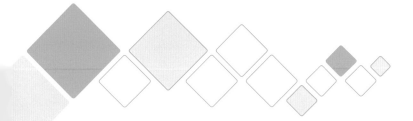

Make a start: The four Rs framework

So far in the preceding pages of this section we have organised the illustrations using the teacher's palette. Below, we show an alternative structure for the quick wins, together with other suggestions, using the framework of the four Rs.

As you get deeper into working on your students' learning power, you will find yourself moving back and forth between the two frameworks — four Rs and teacher's palette. We leave it to you to play with the ideas and the connections between them, and decide how to balance the frameworks in your thinking and planning.

Building resilience

Develop prompts for what to do when you get stuck

Reinforce that having to try hard in learning is not symptomatic of a lack of ability

Set slightly difficult activities which students may have to struggle with

Point out when students are enjoying their learning and help them capture how it feels

Invite students to mind map what distracts them from learning

Building resourcefulness

Recognise and reward good questions as well as good answers

Encourage phrases like 'How come ...?' 'What if ...?' 'How might ...?'

Develop activities that require students to make creative use of a range of resources

Use 'could be' language

Create scenarios for students to visualise or mentally rehearse

Building reflectiveness

Encourage students to anticipate hurdles and obstacles when planning their learning

Create a Learning Wall to display students' own targets and progress as learners

Encourage students to set success criteria and check their own work

Give practice in drawing out the essence of a lesson or experience

Allocate time for students to keep a learning log

Building reciprocity

Get students to develop codes of conduct for working in groups

Divide the class into research teams, each having to find part of the answer

Coach students in the art of good listening

Discuss how we all soak up other people's skills and ideas

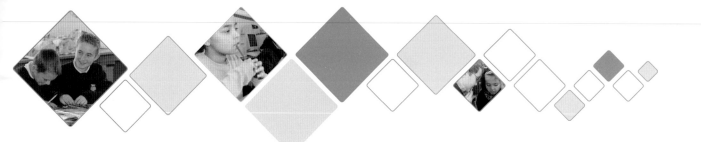

Refine what you do: Watching yourself at work

From self-observation to coaching partnerships

Getting used to looking at the changes in your teaching and the impact on your students is the best way of sustaining your development as a learning-power coach. Coaches use self-observation skills in order to become more reflective and better able to support and challenge the learning of others.

Self-monitoring

Keeping track of the changes you make in the classroom doesn't have to be sophisticated or time consuming. There are some very simple ways of slowing down and getting an objective view of what you are doing. For example, a simple tally chart that logs the number of times you use a particular style of questioning, or mention a particular word, or target a particular individual, can link you into a feedback loop that helps you become more consciously competent.

Reflection

Using a learning log or journal to note down what you have been doing in the classroom — and in your learning life in general — helps you to reflect on your learning and distil useful lessons. Many teachers start a learning journal when starting to introduce learning to learn into their classrooms – usually just a notebook, but it helps if it is big enough for mind maps, flow diagrams and charts as well as simple written notes. They get into the habit of noting down what they have been doing and what they have noticed. This is particularly powerful when done in conjunction with students. You could ask one student in each lesson to monitor an aspect of your performance.

Peer coaching

Once you are in the habit of looking at yourself and asking curious questions, you may – like Sarah – benefit from a coaching partnership with another member of your team. Pairs of colleagues who develop their critical curiosity in a non-judgemental way not only learn from each other, but also hone their observation, listening and questioning skills to the benefit of their work with younger learners.

Tally chart

stopped myself using the question 'why'	卌 |||
rewarded good questions	卌
used 'could be' language		

Your learning log might include:

- brainstorms of ways in which you could start talking differently about learning

- notes on what happened after you changed the room layout to focus on learning to learn

- notes on what happened when you started using the learning wall

- a forcefield analysis of what helps and hinders you in developing students' learning power

- a mind map on how you might take your commentating skills further

- a matrix of exciting activities that you are developing to support different learning capacities

- notes on how you designed activities with twin objectives (learning power and content). A list of things you found difficult in designing these activities

- a plan of what you want to introduce over the next month

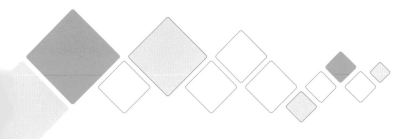

Reflective questions

It is extremely easy in the early stages of introducing learning power to slip into habits that are about less dynamic and long-lasting approaches to learning. The reflective questions alongside should help you to keep focused and on the right track.

Bit by bit, the more you question yourself the more you will consolidate your approaches so that developing your students' learning-power habits becomes second nature to you.

Try exploring these areas

Your questioning

- What ways have you found of asking questions that do not demand justification? (i.e. not asking why?)
- Does this way of asking questions feel comfortable?
- How are your students reacting to new styles of questioning?
- How does this approach make for noticeable improvements in learning?

Using the Learning Wall

- What is the learning wall telling you about students?
- How is it helping students to be clearer about what they can do, and what they need to do to increase their learning power?
- How are students beginning to use each other as a resource for learning?
- How can you develop your use of the learning wall to make it an even more dynamic learning tool?
- What ideas do you have for keeping the learning wall fresh and vibrant?

Talking about learning

- What are you saying that is consistent with the four Rs?
- Have you started to tell less and guide more?
- What effect is this having on students?

The environment

- How does the room layout enable you to consolidate learning to learn more effectively?
- Which of the messages on the walls is having the greatest impact on students' learning approaches?

General

- In what ways are you changing your repertoire as a teacher?
- What is helping or hindering you in keeping your focus specifically on learning power, as opposed to learning in general?
- What evidence do you now have that learning is learnable?

Refine what you do: Collecting student responses

It makes sense to supplement initial reflection on your teaching by enquiring into its impact on your students' behaviour, motivation and achievement.

As we have said previously, you should let your students into the secret of what you are doing, why you are doing it, and the intended outcomes. They will make greater strides towards becoming better learners if you encourage them to be critically curious and to make meaning out of what you are doing together.

Again, your enquiries do not have to be sophisticated or time-consuming, but they will focus your energy and commitment in the classroom once you can see that your efforts are making a difference.

Looking for changes in behaviour

When teachers turn their attention to enhancing students' learning rather than managing behaviour, the results are often striking. Take time to record, for example, the number of disciplinary and admonishing statements that you have to make and the sanctions that you have to employ. Most learning-power teachers find a marked, and sustained, reduction. You might also note the ways in which your students regard, label and address each other, and notice how these things alter from week to week.

Looking for changes in motivation

Remember you are building greater interdependence through your coaching approach to learning. You might look out for improvements in motivation such as higher levels of interest in what they are doing, greater personal responsibility and initiative, recognition of achievement and progress in self and others. Notice ways in which students are becoming less dependent on you.

Looking for changes in achievement

Progress in achievement relates to learning capacities as well as curriculum levels of attainment. You will be able to measure improvements in both of these areas. If you use a baseline survey to profile your students' attitudes and capabilities in respect of the four Rs, you can share progress with them as they expand their learning capacities.

Chart changes in student behaviour

Student behaviour

	Boys	Girls	Wk 1	Wk 2
use of disciplinary comments	⧸⧸⧸⧸ ⏐	⏐⏐⏐	20	15
use of sanctions	⏐⏐⏐⏐	⏐⏐	5	3

Take photographs that catch students extending their learning reach

Chart changes in motivation

	Week 4
Showing greater interest in learning	Simon
	Reuben
Taking more responsibility for learning	Darren
	Ralph
Managing distractions better	Mehmet
Home learning in on time	Katie
	Leyla
Asking more questions	Susie
Showing more confidence	Amin

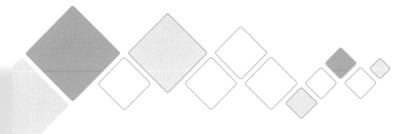

How's my learning power?

Re-checking students' perceptions

After a term or so of working with learning power you might want to get another fix on what your students think about how they are learning. You could use the same questionnaire as you used at the start (pages 8/10). Here are some additional ideas for how you might pose the questions, but again you will want to adapt the language or scoring method to suit your students.

Comparing responses between the first and second questionnaires will enable you to identify those areas which your students perceive that they need to attend to. This may lead you to focus on improving 'listening' or 'distilling' or 'imitation', for example, with the class as a whole or for individuals.

Students reflecting on their learning power

Instruments like the one sketched below invite students to reflect on their learning capacities and to shape targets for improvement. They might find it beneficial to talk the statements through with someone else in the class, and this could lead students to form supportive coaching partnerships. Students will certainly rely on your questioning skills to tease out what they need to do. Talking in positive ways about their learning will help to develop learning muscles.

Read these statements and circle the number that best describes your learning.

I can get so caught up with work that I forget what time it is   Rarely | 1 | 2 | 3 | 4 | Always

I am patient and take time to notice detail   Rarely | 1 | 2 | 3 | 4 | Always

I ask myself questions in order to sort out what I think   Rarely | 1 | 2 | 3 | 4 | Always

I can work things out step by step   Rarely | 1 | 2 | 3 | 4 | Always

I'm good at seeing how things fit together   Rarely | 1 | 2 | 3 | 4 | Always

I know how to plan my work and get things done   Rarely | 1 | 2 | 3 | 4 | Always

I feel OK when I make a mistake   Rarely | 1 | 2 | 3 | 4 | Always

I know how and when I learn at my best   Rarely | 1 | 2 | 3 | 4 | Always

I'm learning a lot by working with other people   Rarely | 1 | 2 | 3 | 4 | Always

I've picked up good learning habits from other people   Rarely | 1 | 2 | 3 | 4 | Always

I listen to other people's ideas carefully   Rarely | 1 | 2 | 3 | 4 | Always

I contribute positively when working in groups   Rarely | 1 | 2 | 3 | 4 | Always

---

Of the four Rs, I think I am most confident with . . . . because I can . . . . . .

The evidence I would use to prove this is that when . . . . . .

Of the four Rs, I think I need to do most work on . . . . because I find the following things difficult

-
-
-

The particular area that I need to work on is . . . . because I find it difficult to . . . .

In order to make a start with this target, I am going to begin by . . . . . .

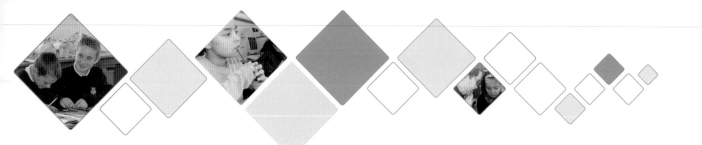

Take things further: Sharpening reactions

Athletes build muscle memory by imagining future scenarios and predicting their reactions. You too can firm up your learning muscles by running through familiar classroom situations in your head, and imagining reacting to them from a learning-power perspective.

Try thinking about the following scenarios with a colleague, and imagine how you would respond as a learning-power coach.

Remember you are trying to become so familiar with learning power approaches that you will respond quickly and naturally with unconscious competence. But beware – don't fall into the trap of thinking that you do all those things already!

1

John is good at maths and he knows it. He works on his own quickly and efficiently. He shows signs of irritation when other people don't understand things as he does. He thinks his teacher isn't as good at maths as he is.

Simon is convinced he can't write. Everything he does is short and thrown together quickly. Although there are weaknesses in his expression, there are signs that he is making links between aspects of work; he has considerable insight that is being hampered by his lack of confidence.

2

Thomas likes to work with Sam but won't allow himself to work with other members of the class – particularly girls. When you try and rearrange the class for group-work he becomes surly and uncooperative, labelling other students as 'thick' and 'stupid'.

4

3

Karen likes to get things right. She works hard at school and always says she's OK and doesn't need help. You sense her homework is often really her Dad's work. You think she doesn't really connect with the basic ideas and that her progress isn't as it should be.

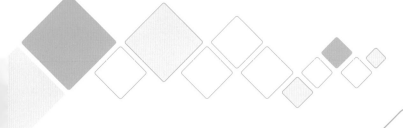

5

Rebecca is producing a piece of project coursework that is satisfactory but would benefit from some revision. You have made some suggestions but she doesn't like to be told and is continuing along her own track because she says, 'That'll do.'

6

Ravi is quiet during a class discussion on rights and responsibilities. When you ask him to say what he thinks, he clams up and says 'I don't know' and 'If that's what you think'. When you ask him to summarise the key points of the discussion he says nothing.

8

Dan doesn't know where to start. You have introduced the work and encouraged use of a range of resources, from the Internet to the school library and classroom assistants. He can't seem to find a focus or starting point.

7

Chloe is easily distracted. She never settles for long without talking to her friends – very often about things unrelated to work in school. At best, she will stay involved with her work for four minutes before her attention wanes.

9

You feel that the class have underdeveloped listening skills. Although they seem to hear your instructions, they often go off at tangents that are not helpful. When you ask them to work together, you don't think they listen to each other and there is often a clamour of competing voices.

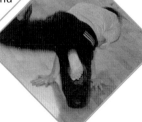

10

Benny asks other students questions that undermine their confidence. He tries to catch them out and make himself seem more capable. You suspect this is because he is quite uncertain himself. A parent has asked you to make sure that her child doesn't work with Benny again.

Look at page 27 to see Sarah's ideas for responding to these situations, when they arose in her classroom.

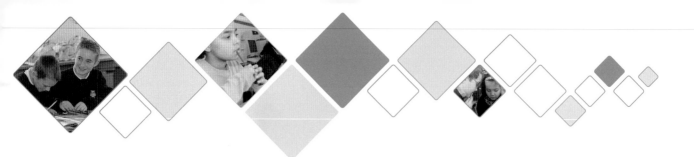

Take things further: Keep track of your ideas

Sarah has used her learning log while working with her students at strengthening their learning power. This page shows her reflecting at the end of a week, quite early in their progress together.

The excerpts on the opposite page are from a little later on: they show how she responded to the situations in her classroom

that we asked you to think about on pages 24 and 25.

These are just two examples of the many ways a learning log can be used. Learning to use one well can stimulate a surprising amount of creative thinking.

Week 5

Success: My classes all used to me using the R words... but I'm sensing irritation
Issue: How to vary the vocab so they don't groan when they hear an R
Action: Live it in my actions and interventions. Use other words - persevere, stick at it, distractions, go with the flow, rapt, engrossed, caught up in, etc

Getting better: I'm learning to interpret messages about what's really going on with the learning - realise how keen students used to be to 'please', so hiding what was really going on. Now being more overt about their difficulties and I am better at picking up the learning capacities they are using.

Simon's using reflective skills to good effect - time invested nudging him on by my questions is paying dividends. His confidence is growing, too as he becomes aware of using the skills.

I'm pleased! Getting everyone to focus on listening and building the skills together has been brilliant. Can't cope with too many things at once......but in fact the students supported each other because they were all doing it - this wasn't happening when I had them all working on different bits.
The proof of the pudding? I haven't heard myself say 'will you listen!' for ages.
Remember! Chunk the learning power development work up more!

Things to remember
- use words meaning 'could be', 'what might', 'when might'
  (need to think up/learn a list)
- think GUIDING
- more day challenges (they really like them)
- find time to work more with Rashid

Things to do
- tape a reminder list to my desk - NOW
- make vocab list (see above!) - end of this week
- re-assess the room layout. Plan a sequence of changes in seating plan
  - by half term
- look for students using the learning wall. Is it helping or does it just make me feel good? - over next 3 weeks

John – develop his ability to coach others?
Ask him to think of ways that might help other students catch on quicker
Ask him to set me challenges to work through in front of the class
Get him to develop a 'what to do when things get tough in maths' chart

Simon – Commentate on his ability to make links – boost his resourcefulness
Provide scaffolding for his writing – alternative ways of recording ideas
Encourage his imaginative skills and track his progress

Karen – Help her to look at herself as a learner – remind her how and when she learns best
Train her in how to capitalise and imitate – not copy
Encourage her to set a target to say 'I don't know' when she doesn't know

Thomas – Remind the class of the need for interdependence in learning
Clarify a role for Thomas when working with others
Suggest he looks at the learning power profiles of all class members so that he can see they all have something to offer

Rebecca – show her examples of work in progress displayed on the wall and the drafts of some writers
Use stilling activities to slow down her process of working
Brainstorm 'what if' and 'could be' alternatives once the work is under way

Ravi – Explore roots of his diffidence – could they be cultural?
Support him in his questioning and reasoning by selecting small-group work
Provide him with some distilling exercises to inform his thinking

Chloe – Spend time with her, looking at her learning capacities – train her to walk away and refresh herself in a socially acceptable way
Give her prompt cards that help her to keep on track
Help her to set her own 'on-task' targets

Dan – Demonstrate the path that you and Dan have taken when starting independent work
Enable a learning assistant to be a resource for him and gradually remove this resource as he grows in confidence
Offer him prompt cards to help him find a focus and evaluate his progress regularly

Class listening skills – Generate ideas about 'what good listening looks like' and get the students to practise coaching each other
Provide activities to remind them about these skills
Frame the ground-rules for collaborative work in groups

Benny – Select activities to support learning positive behaviours
Develop '10 good questions that help other people to learn'
Ask Benny to find five learning habits he wants to imitate from someone else

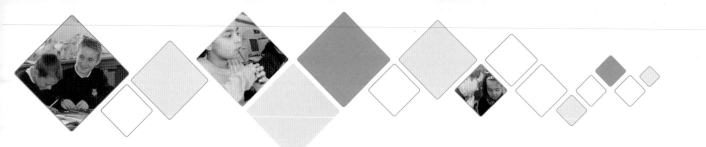

Take things further: What next?

As you establish ways of engaging your students with learning power, you will have the challenge of progressing the ideas and keeping the approach alive and fresh — in terms of both your vitality as a teacher and your students' enthusiasm for continuing to become better learners. Using the prompts below from time to time may help to stimulate the flow of your ideas.

Remember that what is distinctive about learning power is the emphasis on teachers and students consciously engaging together with the details of learning to learn.

Chart your way forward with these prompts:

" I have **had** the following **successes** ... "

" Now I need to **think about** ... "

" I could **try** ... "

" To follow up our first efforts, **I need to** ... "

" I can **make sure** that we don't **get beached (or stuck!) by** ... "

" I can **build progression** into the **four Rs** and **17 capacities by** ... "

" I wonder if **some subjects** are good for sharpening **particular** learning capacities ... "

" **This work could** affect the whole school in ... "

" What help might I benefit from in developing my
    — listening skills?
    — questioning skills?
    — providing constructive feedback?
    — ...? "